G P S

GOAL PLANNING STRATEGY

90-Day

POWER

Journal

Your Companion Handbook to
The GOAL Formula

ERIK THERWANGER

G P S
GOAL PLANNING STRATEGY

90-Day
POWER
Journal

Your Companion Handbook to
The GOAL Formula

The Think**GREAT**® Collection

Published in Prior Lake, Minnesota, by Think GREAT® LLC

The GOAL Formula™ is a trademark of Think GREAT® LLC

Think GREAT® is a registered trademark of Think GREAT® LLC

The GPS: Goal Planning Strategy™ is a trademark of Think GREAT® LLC

ISBN 978-0-9844611-8-9

Library of Congress Subject Headings:

Self-help / Personal Growth / Success

BISAC Subject Headings:

SEL027000   SELF-HELP / Personal Growth / Success

GPS Version 1 – 11-01-14

Dedication

This handbook is dedicated to everyone who has made the commitment to accomplish their goals and enhance their lives. By investing the next 90 days, you are doing more than just achieving greater results in your life; you are empowering others to do the same. You inspire me.

INTRODUCTION

CREATE A SENSE OF URGENCY

The difference between where you are and where you want to be is what you do.

Great Thinker,

Words alone cannot express how excited I am that you are harnessing the power of your *GPS* (Goal Planning Strategy) during your **90 Day Run**. I am more than confident that you will accomplish your goals, which are *life-changing and remarkable in magnitude and degree.*

Your *GPS* will take you beyond merely writing down your goals; it will allow you to focus on the planning and strategy of accomplishing them, no matter what circumstances you face.

The process of setting up your *GPS* is an exciting time. The techniques you learned about by reading my book, *The GOAL Formula™*, will come to life and help you to stay on track with your results as you monitor your performance on a daily basis.

Starting your *GPS* is a great step but continuing to use it throughout your **90 Day Run** will ensure that you stay on course. Remember, the following pages are merely templates for your path to greatness. The most important thing you can do is to take action.

I want to encourage you to go after the life you have always wanted – personally and professionally. As your Goal Coach, I will be with you on your journey!

Think GREAT,

THE GOAL FORMULA

Whether your goals are big or small, life-changing or life-saving, you too can improve your life when you start to *Think GREAT*.

I wrote *The GOAL Formula™* to share my proven techniques for accomplishing goals, during the most challenging circumstances. During my wife's battle with cancer, we focused our attention on our goals as a way to provide us with constant motivation and inspiration.

Designed to help you get started, to stay on track, and to accomplish the goals required for you to achieve a greater life, *The GOAL Formula™* provides the formula necessary for success, personally and professionally. If we were able to do it when we were battling cancer, you can do it too.

Divided into four powerful sections, *The GOAL Formula™* pays careful attention to the parts necessary to get the results you need.

Part I: The Big Picture – Helps you to develop your Big Picture and details the five steps to accomplish any goal.

Part II: Time Mastery – Teaches you how to structure your time, especially during the next 90 days, so you are prepared to complete the big picture of your life.

Part III: You Never Run Alone – Shows you the benefits of incorporating other people into your journey to accomplish your life-changing goals.

Part IV: Your 90 Day Run Starts Now – Provides you an in-depth look at the *GPS* (Goal Planning Strategy), which keeps you on track to see your goals all the way through.

Your *90-Day Power Journal* transforms Part IV into your own *GPS*, allowing you to fully maximize your next 90 days, and accomplish your important goals.

THE FANTASTIC FIVE

Although each goal is unique, they typically fall somewhere into five unique categories (the Fantastic Five). Accomplishing goals in one or more of these areas will help you to have a life that is *remarkable in magnitude and degree*. For most people, their definition of greatness can be found within these five goal categories.

FAITH – Goals that allow you to pursue spiritual growth. Accomplishing Faith goals will allow you to rise beyond the purely material world and find a truer balance in your life.

FAMILY & FRIENDS – Goals that enhance the meaningful relationships in your life. Accomplishing Family & Friends goals will give you a deeper feeling of love and belonging.

FINANCIAL – Goals that involve building a career, increasing income, eliminating debt, and building financial security. Accomplishing Financial goals helps to build stability and gain peace of mind.

FITNESS – Goals that involve improving your health through nutrition and fitness. Accomplishing Fitness goals will help you to live a longer, more enjoyable life.

FUN – Goals that involve your personal interests. Accomplishing your Fun goals will add a new level of excitement to your life.

Imagine how empowered you would feel to accomplish goals within one of these areas! Now imagine accomplishing goals in all of these areas!

When you improve your life in one of these categories, it always gives you the confidence to start improving the others.

Accomplishing life-changing goals always makes life worth living to the fullest. Millions of people are ready to accomplish the goals that will have this amazing impact in their lives, but most of them will never fully prepare themselves for accomplishing them.

Your *GPS* will help you to be prepared for accomplishing life-changing goals.

GOAL PLANNING STRATEGY

Now, it is time to develop your plan on paper. Your *GPS* will give you the framework to establish priorities and to stay on track to accomplish your short-term and long-term goals.

Your *GPS* is much more than just organized words on paper. It is your contract and commitment to yourself; a commitment to improving your life. Max out the power of your *GPS* during your **90 Day Run**.

GOAL: Accomplish goals which are *life-changing and remarkable in magnitude and degree.*

PLANNING: Identify the path to follow in order to achieve greatness.

STRATEGY: Implement your plan, especially when obstacles are in your way.

Your completed *GPS* will be a source of power for your **90 Day Run**. It is your contract and commitment to yourself; a commitment to achieving a greater life. Each day, as you implement and review your personal *GPS*, you will see in full detail:

- Your well-defined short-term and long-term goals
- Pictures of your reasons for accomplishing them
- Your high expectations
- Actions you must take
- Timelines for completion
- Your personal network – people who support your goals
- Communication logs with your great partner
- A daily planner to keep you on track
- Progress reports to measure your success

SUCCESSFULLY COMPLETING YOUR *GPS*

Setting up your Goal Planning Strategy is such an exciting process! Investing time in the development of your *GPS* will ensure that all of the valuable information necessary for a successful **90 Day Run** has been entered.

Your *GPS* will provide you with eight unique components; all designed to work together to help you successfully complete your **90 Day Run**. I have designed the following pages to be a constant source of support, structure, and motivation.

Individual components of your *GPS*:

- Personal Contract
- Overview
- Short-Term Goals
- G.R.E.A.T. Goal Sheet
- Goal Status Sheet
- Daily Action PLanner
- Daily Journal
- GREAT Achievements

As you complete each of the eight components of your *GPS*, be as detailed as possible. A clearly defined *GPS* will help you orchestrate all your actions and create momentum, even before your **90 Day Run** starts! On the following pages, I have provided you with an overview and an example of each component

I will give you one tip: *put your heart into your plan, so your plan can get into your heart.* When your heart and your mind are on the same page, the power of your *GPS* will elevate your ability to accomplish any goal you desire.

STEP 1: PERSONAL CONTRACT

Verbal commitments are fine, but written ones last longer!

Your *Personal Contract* highlights the commitments you are making to yourself and to the completion of your **90 Day Run**. Fill in your name, sign it, and date it. Make copies and post this page on your bathroom mirror, your desk, and in your car as a reminder of your dedication. For added impact, have your GREAT partner sign and date it too. Do the same for your partner.

90-Day Run

PERSONAL CONTRACT

I, _____Erik Therwanger_____ will accomplish my number one goal of completing my **90 Day Run**. I acknowledge that the accomplishment of my goals is extremely important to me and will also have a positive impact on everyone in my life.

I will *Think GREAT* during my entire **90 Day Run**. I will break bad habits and implement great habits. I will be a beacon of positive energy and will strive to inspire others to achieve greatness in their lives.

I understand that my **90 Day Run** will have some challenges, but I will stay persistent and consistent in everything that I do. During my **90 Day Run**, I will control my thoughts and actions. I will eliminate the option of failure.

Most importantly, I will pour my heart into my *GPS*. I will do the same for my GREAT partner. I will commit to reviewing my *GPS* daily and focus my efforts on making my life GREAT!

Erik Therwanger	10/31/2014
My Signature	Date
Gina Therwanger	10/31/2014
My GREAT Partner's Signature	Date

STEP 2: OVERVIEW

Your *Overview* will show the timelines for your **90 Day Run**.

Include your start date and completion date. Your *Overview* is a list of the long-term goals you must accomplish in order to achieve a greater life. Identify which of the "Fantastic Five" categories they fall into. Your long-term goals will be broken down into smaller goals which you will add to the *Short-Term Goals* section.

90-Day Run
OVERVIEW

Start Date: _10/31/2014_   **Completion Date:** _10/31/2014_

In order to achieve a greater life, I will accomplish the following *Long-Term Goals*:

Long-Term Goals	**Fantastic Five**
1. *Eliminate all debt*	*Financial*
2. *Write a Book*	*Fun*
3. *Get in great physical shape*	*Fitness*
4. *Be a better parent*	*Family*
5. *Build a retirement fund*	*Financial*

My Great Partner: _Gina Therwanger_

Communication Sessions

Daily (Time): _8:00 pm_

Weekly (Day): _Saturday_   **Time:** _3:30 pm_

STEP 3: SHORT-TERM GOALS

Use your *Short-Term Goals* section to identify all of the personal goals you will accomplish during your **90 Day Run**. Add in any of the shared goals that you and your partner want to accomplish together. Once again, list which of the "Fantastic Five" categories they fall into. Avoid the mistake of trying to tackle too many goals at the same time.

Do not forget to list your first goal as "Complete My **90 Day Run!**"

90-Day Run
SHORT-TERM GOALS

Personal Goals — **Fantastic Five**

1. COMPLETE MY 90 DAY RUN —
2. Complete one chapter of my book per month — Fun
3. Plan three family outings — Family
4. Meet with a Financial Planner — Financial
5. Lose 25 pounds — Fitness

Shared Goals — **Fantastic Five**

1. Plan a "Date-Night" once per month — Family
2. Find a long-term Financial Planner — Financial
3. Pay off credit card - $4,200 — Financial
4. Build a savings account - $1,000 — Financial
5. ___ — ___

STEP 4: G.R.E.A.T. GOAL SHEET

Transfer each of your *Short-Term Goals* to an individual *G.R.E.A.T. Goal Sheet* and list all of the information associated with each specific goal you expect to accomplish during your **90 Day Run**. Be specific and and provide as much detail as possible.

90-Day Run
G.R.E.A.T. GOAL SHEET #1

Goal #1: *Lose 25 pounds.*

Reasons: *I want to lose this weight so I feel better and look better.*
I want to live longer and be able to have the energy to do more with my wife and kids.

Expectations: *I will not give up. I will push myself everyday to stay on track.*
I will make my meals the night before so I don't have the need to buy fast food.

Actions: *I will eat three healthy meals each day and I will have three small snacks*
in between meals to keep my metabolism going.
I will exercise each day.

Tracking: *I will track my meals and exercise regimen each night using my Daily Action Planner.*
I will track my results each week by weighing in daily!!!!

STEP 5: GOAL STATUS SHEET

This is where you will track your results and measure your progress for each of your short-term goals. This will require you to keep track of how close you are to the completion of your goal by using the "% Complete" thermometer.

—— *90-Day Run* ——

GOAL STATUS SHEET #1

Goal #1: Lose 25 pounds

Timeline for Completion: 10/31/2014 – 75 Days

I commit to eliminating these habits:

Eating fast food, drinking soda, eating late at night, being a couch potato.

I commit to adding these habits:

Preparing healthy meals each night for the following day, take vitamins daily,

exercise daily, and get enough sleep.

```
100%
 90%
 80%        %          Personal Network:
 70%     COMPLETE         Louis B.
 60%                      Kelli N.
                          Charlie H.
```

STEP 6: DAILY ACTION PLANNER

Each day represents just over 1% of your **90 Day Run**. Account for both your day-to-day, and your goal-related actions. For your day-to-day actions, put a "D" under Type. For your goal-related actions, put a "G" under Type. By identifying the type of actions that occupy your day, you will discover ways to convert some of your day-to-day actions into goal-related actions: "D+G." Avoid making your *Daily Action Planner* a "To Do List."

Allocate time for "Single" actions (completed once during your 90 Day Run) and "Multiple" actions (repeated throughout your 90 Day Run).

90-Day Run

GOAL STATUS SHEET #1

DAY 01

	Time	Multiple Action Items	Type	Done
1.	7:30 am	Take the kids to school	D	☑
2.	8:30 am	Start work	D	☑
3.	12:30 pm	Eat a healthy lunch	D+G	☑
4.	6:00 pm	Eat a healthy dinner with the family	D+G	☑
5.	8:00 pm	Review GPS with my Great partner	G	☑
6.	8:30 pm	Exercise	G	☑
7.	9:00 pm	Prepare meals for the following day	G	☑
8.	9:30 pm	Put the kids to bed	D	☑
9.	9:45 pm	Write a couple pages in my book	G	☐
10.	10:30 pm	Go to bed	D+G	☑
11.				☐
12.				☐
13.				☐
14.				☐
15.				☐

	Time	Single Action Items	Type	Done
1.	1:00 pm	Schedule appointment with financial planner	G	☑
2.	1:15 pm	Pay bills -- send $250 extra to credit card	D+G	☑
3.				☐
4.				☐
5.				☐

STEP 7: DAILY JOURNAL

The longer you make daily entries consistently, the greater the benefits are to your **90 Day Run**. A *Daily Journal* keeps you pro-active and is a reminder of how serious your goals are to you. I have found that when you stop your journal entries, you soon stop your program. Your Journal allows you to keep track of your strengths and weaknesses.

A motivational excerpt from *The GOAL Formula™*, will be on each page of your *Daily Journal* to inspire you!

90-Day Run

DAILY JOURNAL

DAY 01

Strengths: I stayed on track with my schedule about 95%.
Exercised on time and ate healthy meals. Spoke with my Great Partner for 15 minutes.

Weaknesses: Ate lunch later than I wanted. Did not write any pages tonight.
I got home late from work and missed eating dinner with family.

How I can improve: I will make up for the missed pages this weekend.
I will catch up at work to avoid missing any more goal-related actions!

GREAT thoughts for today: It was great taking action towards my goals today.
Speaking to Gina about our GPS gave both of us a tremendous boost of power.
I feel my confidence level growing.

Think GREAT today:
Do not just sit back and watch others achieve greatness.
Think GREAT and achieve it in your own life!

STEP 8: GREAT ACHIEVEMENTS

Congratulations, you have successfully completed a life-changing step toward a greater life!

Each time you accomplish one of your goals, write it down on this form. It is time to celebrate!

90-Day Run

GREAT ACHIEVEMENTS

Congratulations!

	GOAL	DATE COMPLETED
1.	Picked our financial planner	11/10/2014
2.	Took family trip to the beach	11/13/2014
3.	Set up retirement fund	11/17/2014
4.	Completed first chapter of my book	11/27/2014
5.	Took family trip to amusement park	12/13/2014
6.	Completed second chapter of my book	12/24/2014
7.		
8.		
9.		
10.		

GREAT job!

90 DAY CALENDAR – COUNTDOWN TO GREATNESS

I have always found great strength and motivation in using a countdown calendar whenever I am on a **90 Day Run**. I love the power of this visual aid to identify how many days I have completed and how many days I have to go. I have created a Countdown Calendar for you at the back of this workbook to use during your **90 Day Run**. Thinking great is always about thinking differently, so we will go beyond just merely crossing off each day as it goes by.

Let each mark on your calendar represent how well you did on that particular day. What works for me is to use the following shapes to indicate how closely I stayed on target with my greater purpose, by completing all of my activities.

X – X marks the spot! You completed 100% of your activities for the day! You seized the day! GREAT Job!

M – M is for most. You completed over 50% of your activities, but fell short of 100%. You put in a great effort, but will shoot for the X tomorrow.

O – Oh No! The day got away from you and you completed less than 50% of your activities. You will do better tomorrow!

Example:

Remember, your **90 Day Run** is not about chasing perfection. It is about staying consistent and course-correcting along the way. Use your Countdown Calendar on the next page as a visual motivator. Shoot for an "X" every day. If you get an "M" or an "O", review your journal page for that day and determine how you can improve.

90-Day Run Countdown Calendar

Day 01	Day 02	Day 03	Day 04	Day 05	Day 06	Day 07
Day 08	Day 09	Day 10	Day 11	Day 12	Day 13	Day 14
Day 15	Day 16	Day 17	Day 18	Day 19	Day 20	Day 21
Day 22	Day 23	Day 24	Day 25	Day 26	Day 27	Day 28
Day 29	Day 30	Day 31	Day 32	Day 33	Day 34	Day 35
Day 36	Day 37	Day 38	Day 39	Day 40	Day 41	Day 42
Day 43	Day 44	Day 45	Day 46	Day 47	Day 48	Day 49
Day 50	Day 51	Day 52	Day 53	Day 54	Day 55	Day 56
Day 57	Day 58	Day 59	Day 60	Day 61	Day 62	Day 63
Day 64	Day 65	Day 66	Day 67	Day 68	Day 69	Day 70
Day 71	Day 72	Day 73	Day 74	Day 75	Day 76	Day 77
Day 78	Day 79	Day 80	Day 81	Day 82	Day 83	Day 84
Day 85	Day 86	Day 87	Day 88	Day 89	Day 90	

90-Day Run

PERSONAL CONTRACT

I, _____ will accomplish

my number one goal of completing my **90 Day Run**. I acknowledge that

the accomplishment of my goals is extremely important to me and will

also have a positive impact on everyone in my life.

I will *Think GREAT* during my entire **90 Day Run**. I will break bad habits

and implement great habits. I will be a beacon of positive energy and

will strive to inspire others to achieve greatness in their lives.

I understand that my **90 Day Run** will have some challenges, but I will

stay persistent and consistent in everything that I do. During my **90 Day

Run**, I will control my thoughts and actions. I will eliminate the option of

failure.

Most importantly, I will pour my heart into my *GPS*. I will do the same

for my GREAT partner. I will commit to reviewing my *GPS* daily and focus

my efforts on making my life GREAT!

_____   _____
My Signature   Date

_____   _____
My GREAT Partner's Signature   Date

90-Day Run

OVERVIEW

Start Date: _____   **Completion Date:** _____

In order to achieve a greater life, I will accomplish the following
Long-Term Goals:

Long-Term Goals		**Fantastic Five**
1.	_____	_____
2.	_____	_____
3.	_____	_____
4.	_____	_____
5.	_____	_____

My Great Partner: _____

Communication Sessions

Daily (Time): _____

Weekly (Day): _____   **Time:** _____

SHORT-TERM GOALS

Personal Goals   **Fantastic Five**

1. _____   _____

2. _____   _____

3. _____   _____

4. _____   _____

5. _____   _____

Shared Goals   **Fantastic Five**

1. _____   _____

2. _____   _____

3. _____   _____

4. _____   _____

5. _____   _____

G.R.E.A.T. GOAL SHEET #1

Goal #1: _____

Reasons: _____

_____

_____

_____

Expectations: _____

_____

_____

_____

Actions: _____

_____

_____

_____

Tracking: _____

_____

_____

_____

90-Day Run

GOAL STATUS SHEET #1

Goal #1: _____

Timeline for Completion: _____

I commit to eliminating these habits:

_____
_____
_____

I commit to adding these habits:

_____
_____
_____

100%
90%
80%
70%
60%
50%
40%
30%
20%
10%

% COMPLETE

Personal Network:

_____
_____
_____
_____
_____

5

90-Day Run

G.R.E.A.T. GOAL SHEET #2

Goal #2: _____

Reasons: _____
_____
_____
_____

Expectations: _____
_____
_____
_____

Actions: _____
_____
_____
_____

Tracking: _____
_____
_____
_____

GOAL STATUS SHEET #2

Goal #2: _____

Timeline for Completion: _____

I commit to eliminating these habits:

_____

_____

_____

I commit to adding these habits:

_____

_____

_____

100%
90%
80%
70%
60%
50%
40%
30%
20%
10%

%
COMPLETE

Personal Network:

_____

_____

_____

_____

_____

90-Day Run

G.R.E.A.T. GOAL SHEET #3

Goal #3: _____

Reasons: _____
_____
_____
_____

Expectations: _____
_____
_____
_____

Actions: _____
_____
_____
_____

Tracking: _____
_____
_____
_____

GOAL STATUS SHEET #3

Goal #3: _____

Timeline for Completion: _____

I commit to eliminating these habits:

_____

_____

_____

I commit to adding these habits:

_____

_____

_____

| 100% |
| 90% |
| 80% |
| 70% |
| 60% |
| 50% |
| 40% |
| 30% |
| 20% |
| 10% |

% COMPLETE

Personal Network:

_____

_____

_____

_____

_____

G.R.E.A.T. GOAL SHEET #4

Goal #4: _____

Reasons: _____

_____

_____

_____

Expectations: _____

_____

_____

_____

Actions: _____

_____

_____

_____

Tracking: _____

_____

_____

_____

GOAL STATUS SHEET #4

Goal #4: _____

Timeline for Completion: _____

I commit to eliminating these habits:

_____

_____

_____

I commit to adding these habits:

_____

_____

_____

100%
90%
80%
70%
60%
50%
40%
30%
20%
10%

%
COMPLETE

Personal Network:

_____

_____

_____

_____

_____

G.R.E.A.T. GOAL SHEET #5

Goal #5: _____

Reasons: _____

_____

_____

_____

Expectations: _____

_____

_____

_____

Actions: _____

_____

_____

_____

Tracking: _____

_____

_____

_____

GOAL STATUS SHEET #5

Goal #5: _____

Timeline for Completion: _____

I commit to eliminating these habits:

_____

_____

_____

I commit to adding these habits:

_____

_____

_____

| 100% |
| 90% |
| 80% |
| 70% |
| 60% |
| 50% |
| 40% |
| 30% |
| 20% |
| 10% |

%
COMPLETE

Personal Network:

_____

_____

_____

_____

_____

DAILY ACTION PLANNER

DAY
01

	Time	*Multiple* Action Items	Type	Done
1.				☐
2.				☐
3.				☐
4.				☐
5.				☐
6.				☐
7.				☐
8.				☐
9.				☐
10.				☐

	Time	*Single* Action Items	Type	Done
1.				☐
2.				☐
3.				☐

90-Day Run

JOURNAL

DAY
01

Strengths: _____

_____

_____

Weaknesses: _____

_____

_____

How I Can Improve: _____

_____

_____

GREAT thoughts for today: _____

_____

_____

Think GREAT Today:

Do not just sit back and watch others achieve greatness.
Think GREAT and achieve it in your own life.

90-Day Run

DAILY ACTION PLANNER

DAY
02

	Time	*Multiple* Action Items	Type	Done
1.				☐
2.				☐
3.				☐
4.				☐
5.				☐
6.				☐
7.				☐
8.				☐
9.				☐
10.				☐

	Time	*Single* Action Items	Type	Done
1.				☐
2.				☐
3.				☐

90-Day Run

JOURNAL

DAY
02

Strengths: _____

_____

_____

Weaknesses: _____

_____

_____

How I Can Improve: _____

_____

_____

GREAT thoughts for today: _____

_____

_____

Think GREAT Today:

Now is the best time to start thinking great.

90-Day Run

DAILY ACTION PLANNER

DAY
03

	Time	*Multiple* Action Items	Type	Done
1.				☐
2.				☐
3.				☐
4.				☐
5.				☐
6.				☐
7.				☐
8.				☐
9.				☐
10.				☐

	Time	*Single* Action Items	Type	Done
1.				☐
2.				☐
3.				☐

90-Day Run

JOURNAL

DAY 03

Strengths: _____

_____

_____

Weaknesses: _____

_____

_____

How I Can Improve: _____

_____

_____

GREAT thoughts for today: _____

_____

_____

Think GREAT Today:

If you want to change some things in your life,
you need to change some things in your life.

90-Day Run

DAILY ACTION PLANNER

DAY
04

	Time	*Multiple* Action Items	Type	Done
1.				☐
2.				☐
3.				☐
4.				☐
5.				☐
6.				☐
7.				☐
8.				☐
9.				☐
10.				☐

	Time	*Single* Action Items	Type	Done
1.				☐
2.				☐
3.				☐

90-Day Run

JOURNAL

DAY
04

Strengths: _____

_____

_____

Weaknesses: _____

_____

_____

How I Can Improve: _____

_____

_____

GREAT thoughts for today: _____

_____

_____

Think GREAT Today:

By choosing to have a greater life,
you will begin to lay the foundation for greatness.

90-Day Run

DAILY ACTION PLANNER

DAY
05

	Time	*Multiple* Action Items	Type	Done
1.	___	_____	___	☐
2.	___	_____	___	☐
3.	___	_____	___	☐
4.	___	_____	___	☐
5.	___	_____	___	☐
6.	___	_____	___	☐
7.	___	_____	___	☐
8.	___	_____	___	☐
9.	___	_____	___	☐
10.	___	_____	___	☐

	Time	*Single* Action Items	Type	Done
1.	___	_____	___	☐
2.	___	_____	___	☐
3.	___	_____	___	☐

90-Day Run

JOURNAL

DAY
05

Strengths: _____

_____

_____

Weaknesses: _____

_____

_____

How I Can Improve: _____

_____

_____

GREAT thoughts for today: _____

_____

_____

Think GREAT Today:

Make the commitment to make the most of your journey,
all the way from Point A to Point B.

90-Day Run

DAILY ACTION PLANNER

DAY
06

	Time	*Multiple* Action Items	Type	Done
1.	_____	_____	_____	☐
2.	_____	_____	_____	☐
3.	_____	_____	_____	☐
4.	_____	_____	_____	☐
5.	_____	_____	_____	☐
6.	_____	_____	_____	☐
7.	_____	_____	_____	☐
8.	_____	_____	_____	☐
9.	_____	_____	_____	☐
10.	_____	_____	_____	☐

	Time	*Single* Action Items	Type	Done
1.	_____	_____	_____	☐
2.	_____	_____	_____	☐
3.	_____	_____	_____	☐

90-Day Run

DAY
06

Strengths: _____

_____

_____

Weaknesses: _____

_____

_____

How I Can Improve: _____

_____

_____

GREAT thoughts for today: _____

_____

_____

Think GREAT Today:

Make the decision to look beyond your obstacles.

90-Day Run

DAILY ACTION PLANNER

DAY
07

	Time	*Multiple* Action Items	Type	Done
1.	_____	_____	_____	☐
2.	_____	_____	_____	☐
3.	_____	_____	_____	☐
4.	_____	_____	_____	☐
5.	_____	_____	_____	☐
6.	_____	_____	_____	☐
7.	_____	_____	_____	☐
8.	_____	_____	_____	☐
9.	_____	_____	_____	☐
10.	_____	_____	_____	☐

	Time	*Single* Action Items	Type	Done
1.	_____	_____	_____	☐
2.	_____	_____	_____	☐
3.	_____	_____	_____	☐

90-Day Run

JOURNAL

DAY
07

Strengths: _____

_____

_____

Weaknesses: _____

_____

_____

How I Can Improve: _____

_____

_____

GREAT thoughts for today: _____

_____

_____

Think GREAT Today:

*Stay laser-focused during your first three weeks and you
will set new patterns and habits.*

90-Day Run

DAILY ACTION PLANNER

DAY
08

	Time	*Multiple* Action Items	Type	Done
1.	_____	_____	_____	☐
2.	_____	_____	_____	☐
3.	_____	_____	_____	☐
4.	_____	_____	_____	☐
5.	_____	_____	_____	☐
6.	_____	_____	_____	☐
7.	_____	_____	_____	☐
8.	_____	_____	_____	☐
9.	_____	_____	_____	☐
10.	_____	_____	_____	☐

	Time	*Single* Action Items	Type	Done
1.	_____	_____	_____	☐
2.	_____	_____	_____	☐
3.	_____	_____	_____	☐

JOURNAL

DAY
08

Strengths: _____

_____

_____

Weaknesses: _____

_____

_____

How I Can Improve: _____

_____

_____

GREAT thoughts for today: _____

_____

_____

Think GREAT Today:

*Today, make a point to tell people something
great about themselves.*

90-Day Run

DAILY ACTION PLANNER

DAY
09

	Time	*Multiple* Action Items	Type	Done
1.				☐
2.				☐
3.				☐
4.				☐
5.				☐
6.				☐
7.				☐
8.				☐
9.				☐
10.				☐

	Time	*Single* Action Items	Type	Done
1.				☐
2.				☐
3.				☐

90-Day Run

JOURNAL

DAY
09

Strengths: _____

_____

_____

Weaknesses: _____

_____

_____

How I Can Improve: _____

_____

_____

GREAT thoughts for today: _____

_____

_____

Think GREAT Today:

Do not let today be average.

90-Day Run

DAILY ACTION PLANNER

DAY
10

	Time	*Multiple* Action Items	Type	Done
1.				☐
2.				☐
3.				☐
4.				☐
5.				☐
6.				☐
7.				☐
8.				☐
9.				☐
10.				☐

	Time	*Single* Action Items	Type	Done
1.				☐
2.				☐
3.				☐

90-Day Run

JOURNAL

DAY
10

Strengths: _____

_____

_____

Weaknesses: _____

_____

_____

How I Can Improve: _____

_____

_____

GREAT thoughts for today: _____

_____

_____

Think GREAT Today:

Accomplishing life-changing goals always
makes life worth living to the fullest.

90-Day Run

DAILY ACTION PLANNER

DAY
11

	Time	*Multiple* Action Items	Type	Done
1.				☐
2.				☐
3.				☐
4.				☐
5.				☐
6.				☐
7.				☐
8.				☐
9.				☐
10.				☐

	Time	*Single* Action Items	Type	Done
1.				☐
2.				☐
3.				☐

90-Day Run

JOURNAL

DAY
11

Strengths: _____

_____

_____

Weaknesses: _____

_____

_____

How I Can Improve: _____

_____

_____

GREAT thoughts for today: _____

_____

_____

Think GREAT Today:

Long-term goals help you to overcome short-term obstacles.

90-Day Run

DAILY ACTION PLANNER

DAY
12

	Time	*Multiple* Action Items	Type	Done
1.				☐
2.				☐
3.				☐
4.				☐
5.				☐
6.				☐
7.				☐
8.				☐
9.				☐
10.				☐

	Time	*Single* Action Items	Type	Done
1.				☐
2.				☐
3.				☐

90-Day Run

JOURNAL

DAY
12

Strengths: _____

_____

_____

Weaknesses: _____

_____

_____

How I Can Improve: _____

_____

_____

GREAT thoughts for today: _____

_____

_____

Think GREAT Today:

Accomplishing goals in one area of your life,
will have a positive effect in other areas.

90-Day Run

DAILY ACTION PLANNER

DAY
13

	Time	*Multiple* Action Items	Type	Done
1.	_____	_____	_____	☐
2.	_____	_____	_____	☐
3.	_____	_____	_____	☐
4.	_____	_____	_____	☐
5.	_____	_____	_____	☐
6.	_____	_____	_____	☐
7.	_____	_____	_____	☐
8.	_____	_____	_____	☐
9.	_____	_____	_____	☐
10.	_____	_____	_____	☐

	Time	*Single* Action Items	Type	Done
1.	_____	_____	_____	☐
2.	_____	_____	_____	☐
3.	_____	_____	_____	☐

90-Day Run

JOURNAL

DAY
13

Strengths: _____

_____

_____

Weaknesses: _____

_____

_____

How I Can Improve: _____

_____

_____

GREAT thoughts for today: _____

_____

_____

Think GREAT Today:

*By making your life greater, you will empower
others to do the same.*

90-Day Run

DAILY ACTION PLANNER

DAY
14

	Time	*Multiple* Action Items	Type	Done
1.	_____	_____	_____	☐
2.	_____	_____	_____	☐
3.	_____	_____	_____	☐
4.	_____	_____	_____	☐
5.	_____	_____	_____	☐
6.	_____	_____	_____	☐
7.	_____	_____	_____	☐
8.	_____	_____	_____	☐
9.	_____	_____	_____	☐
10.	_____	_____	_____	☐

	Time	*Single* Action Items	Type	Done
1.	_____	_____	_____	☐
2.	_____	_____	_____	☐
3.	_____	_____	_____	☐

90-Day Run

JOURNAL

DAY
14

Strengths: _____

_____

_____

Weaknesses: _____

_____

_____

How I Can Improve: _____

_____

_____

GREAT thoughts for today: _____

_____

_____

Think GREAT Today:

A greater life is rarely achieved in your "comfort zone."

DAILY ACTION PLANNER

DAY
15

	Time	*Multiple* Action Items	Type	Done
1.				☐
2.				☐
3.				☐
4.				☐
5.				☐
6.				☐
7.				☐
8.				☐
9.				☐
10.				☐

	Time	*Single* Action Items	Type	Done
1.				☐
2.				☐
3.				☐

90-Day Run

JOURNAL

DAY
15

Strengths: _____

_____

_____

Weaknesses: _____

_____

_____

How I Can Improve: _____

_____

_____

GREAT thoughts for today: _____

_____

_____

Think GREAT Today:

You do not have to wait until your goal is
accomplished to start experiencing the benefits.

90-Day Run

DAILY ACTION PLANNER

DAY
16

	Time	*Multiple* Action Items	Type	Done
1.				☐
2.				☐
3.				☐
4.				☐
5.				☐
6.				☐
7.				☐
8.				☐
9.				☐
10.				☐

	Time	*Single* Action Items	Type	Done
1.				☐
2.				☐
3.				☐

90-Day Run

JOURNAL

DAY
16

Strengths: _____

_____

_____

Weaknesses: _____

_____

_____

How I Can Improve: _____

_____

_____

GREAT thoughts for today: _____

_____

_____

Think GREAT Today:

Success and failure are both options.
Choose success!

90-Day Run

DAILY ACTION PLANNER

DAY
17

	Time	*Multiple* Action Items	Type	Done
1.				☐
2.				☐
3.				☐
4.				☐
5.				☐
6.				☐
7.				☐
8.				☐
9.				☐
10.				☐

	Time	*Single* Action Items	Type	Done
1.				☐
2.				☐
3.				☐

90-Day Run

JOURNAL

DAY
17

Strengths: _____

_____

_____

Weaknesses: _____

_____

_____

How I Can Improve: _____

_____

_____

GREAT thoughts for today: _____

_____

_____

Think GREAT Today:

Your goals are defined dreams with a powerful plan.

DAILY ACTION PLANNER

DAY
18

	Time	*Multiple* Action Items	Type	Done
1.				☐
2.				☐
3.				☐
4.				☐
5.				☐
6.				☐
7.				☐
8.				☐
9.				☐
10.				☐

	Time	*Single* Action Items	Type	Done
1.				☐
2.				☐
3.				☐

90-Day Run

JOURNAL

DAY
18

Strengths: _____

_____

_____

Weaknesses: _____

_____

_____

How I Can Improve: _____

_____

_____

GREAT thoughts for today: _____

_____

_____

Think GREAT Today:

The moment you begin to work on your goals,
you begin to improve your life.

DAILY ACTION PLANNER

DAY
19

	Time	*Multiple* Action Items	Type	Done
1.				☐
2.				☐
3.				☐
4.				☐
5.				☐
6.				☐
7.				☐
8.				☐
9.				☐
10.				☐

	Time	*Single* Action Items	Type	Done
1.				☐
2.				☐
3.				☐

90-Day Run

JOURNAL

DAY
19

Strengths: _____

_____

_____

Weaknesses: _____

_____

_____

How I Can Improve: _____

_____

_____

GREAT thoughts for today: _____

_____

_____

Think GREAT Today:

Important goals provide hope.

90-Day Run

DAILY ACTION PLANNER

DAY
20

	Time	*Multiple* Action Items	Type	Done
1.				☐
2.				☐
3.				☐
4.				☐
5.				☐
6.				☐
7.				☐
8.				☐
9.				☐
10.				☐

	Time	*Single* Action Items	Type	Done
1.				☐
2.				☐
3.				☐

90-Day Run

JOURNAL

DAY
20

Strengths: _____

_____

_____

Weaknesses: _____

_____

_____

How I Can Improve: _____

_____

_____

GREAT thoughts for today: _____

_____

_____

Think GREAT Today:

Striving toward your goals will build your self-esteem.

90-Day Run

DAILY ACTION PLANNER

DAY
21

	Time	*Multiple* Action Items	Type	Done
1.				☐
2.				☐
3.				☐
4.				☐
5.				☐
6.				☐
7.				☐
8.				☐
9.				☐
10.				☐

	Time	*Single* Action Items	Type	Done
1.				☐
2.				☐
3.				☐

90-Day Run

JOURNAL

DAY
21

Strengths: _____

_____

_____

Weaknesses: _____

_____

_____

How I Can Improve: _____

_____

_____

GREAT thoughts for today: _____

_____

_____

Think GREAT Today:

When you focus on a greater life,
you look forward to what each day will bring.

90-Day Run

DAILY ACTION PLANNER

DAY
22

Time	*Multiple* Action Items	Type	Done
1. ___	_____	___	☐
2. ___	_____	___	☐
3. ___	_____	___	☐
4. ___	_____	___	☐
5. ___	_____	___	☐
6. ___	_____	___	☐
7. ___	_____	___	☐
8. ___	_____	___	☐
9. ___	_____	___	☐
10. ___	_____	___	☐

Time	*Single* Action Items	Type	Done
1. ___	_____	___	☐
2. ___	_____	___	☐
3. ___	_____	___	☐

90-Day Run

JOURNAL

DAY
22

Strengths: _____

_____

_____

Weaknesses: _____

_____

_____

How I Can Improve: _____

_____

_____

GREAT thoughts for today: _____

_____

_____

Think GREAT Today:

*Focusing on your goals automatically improves
your performance in other areas of your life.*

90-Day Run

DAILY ACTION PLANNER

DAY
23

	Time	*Multiple* Action Items	Type	Done
1.				☐
2.				☐
3.				☐
4.				☐
5.				☐
6.				☐
7.				☐
8.				☐
9.				☐
10.				☐

	Time	*Single* Action Items	Type	Done
1.				☐
2.				☐
3.				☐

90-Day Run

JOURNAL

DAY
23

Strengths: _____

_____

_____

Weaknesses: _____

_____

_____

How I Can Improve: _____

_____

_____

GREAT thoughts for today: _____

_____

_____

Think GREAT Today:

When is good not good enough?
When your life can be GREAT!

90-Day Run

DAILY ACTION PLANNER

DAY
24

	Time	*Multiple* Action Items	Type	Done
1.				☐
2.				☐
3.				☐
4.				☐
5.				☐
6.				☐
7.				☐
8.				☐
9.				☐
10.				☐

	Time	*Single* Action Items	Type	Done
1.				☐
2.				☐
3.				☐

90-Day Run

JOURNAL

DAY
24

Strengths: _____

_____

_____

Weaknesses: _____

_____

_____

How I Can Improve: _____

_____

_____

GREAT thoughts for today: _____

_____

_____

Think GREAT Today:

*You have the ability to make a significant impact
in your own life.*

90-Day Run

DAILY ACTION PLANNER

DAY
25

	Time	*Multiple* Action Items	Type	Done
1.				☐
2.				☐
3.				☐
4.				☐
5.				☐
6.				☐
7.				☐
8.				☐
9.				☐
10.				☐

	Time	*Single* Action Items	Type	Done
1.				☐
2.				☐
3.				☐

90-Day Run

JOURNAL

DAY
25

Strengths: _____

_____

_____

Weaknesses: _____

_____

_____

How I Can Improve: _____

_____

_____

GREAT thoughts for today: _____

_____

_____

Think GREAT Today:

Today, you are transforming your life.

DAILY ACTION PLANNER

DAY
26

	Time	*Multiple* Action Items	Type	Done
1.				☐
2.				☐
3.				☐
4.				☐
5.				☐
6.				☐
7.				☐
8.				☐
9.				☐
10.				☐

	Time	*Single* Action Items	Type	Done
1.				☐
2.				☐
3.				☐

90-Day Run

JOURNAL

DAY
26

Strengths: _____

_____

_____

Weaknesses: _____

_____

_____

How I Can Improve: _____

_____

_____

GREAT thoughts for today: _____

_____

_____

Think GREAT Today:

Success leaves clues, if you are looking for them.

90-Day Run

DAILY ACTION PLANNER

DAY
27

	Time	*Multiple* Action Items	Type	Done
1.				☐
2.				☐
3.				☐
4.				☐
5.				☐
6.				☐
7.				☐
8.				☐
9.				☐
10.				☐

	Time	*Single* Action Items	Type	Done
1.				☐
2.				☐
3.				☐

90-Day Run

JOURNAL

DAY
27

Strengths: _____

_____

_____

Weaknesses: _____

_____

_____

How I Can Improve: _____

_____

_____

GREAT thoughts for today: _____

_____

_____

Think GREAT Today:

Goals give you an edge.

90-Day Run

DAILY ACTION PLANNER

DAY
28

	Time	*Multiple* Action Items	Type	Done
1.	_____	_____	_____	☐
2.	_____	_____	_____	☐
3.	_____	_____	_____	☐
4.	_____	_____	_____	☐
5.	_____	_____	_____	☐
6.	_____	_____	_____	☐
7.	_____	_____	_____	☐
8.	_____	_____	_____	☐
9.	_____	_____	_____	☐
10.	_____	_____	_____	☐

	Time	*Single* Action Items	Type	Done
1.	_____	_____	_____	☐
2.	_____	_____	_____	☐
3.	_____	_____	_____	☐

90-Day Run

JOURNAL

DAY
28

Strengths: _____

_____

_____

Weaknesses: _____

_____

_____

How I Can Improve: _____

_____

_____

GREAT thoughts for today: _____

_____

_____

Think GREAT Today:

*Stop focusing on what others think
and start Thinking GREAT!*

90-Day Run

DAILY ACTION PLANNER

DAY
29

	Time	*Multiple* Action Items	Type	Done
1.				☐
2.				☐
3.				☐
4.				☐
5.				☐
6.				☐
7.				☐
8.				☐
9.				☐
10.				☐

	Time	*Single* Action Items	Type	Done
1.				☐
2.				☐
3.				☐

90-Day Run

JOURNAL

DAY
29

Strengths: _____

_____

_____

Weaknesses: _____

_____

_____

How I Can Improve: _____

_____

_____

GREAT thoughts for today: _____

_____

_____

Think GREAT Today:

There is only one purpose for setting goals...
to accomplish them.

90-Day Run

DAILY ACTION PLANNER

DAY
30

	Time	*Multiple* Action Items	Type	Done
1.				☐
2.				☐
3.				☐
4.				☐
5.				☐
6.				☐
7.				☐
8.				☐
9.				☐
10.				☐

	Time	*Single* Action Items	Type	Done
1.				☐
2.				☐
3.				☐

90-Day Run

JOURNAL

DAY
30

Strengths: _____

_____

_____

Weaknesses: _____

_____

_____

How I Can Improve: _____

_____

_____

GREAT thoughts for today: _____

_____

_____

Think GREAT Today:

As you accomplish your goals, you transform your life
from "settling" to "soaring."

90-Day Run

DAILY ACTION PLANNER

DAY
31

	Time	*Multiple* Action Items	Type	Done
1.	_____	_____	_____	☐
2.	_____	_____	_____	☐
3.	_____	_____	_____	☐
4.	_____	_____	_____	☐
5.	_____	_____	_____	☐
6.	_____	_____	_____	☐
7.	_____	_____	_____	☐
8.	_____	_____	_____	☐
9.	_____	_____	_____	☐
10.	_____	_____	_____	☐

	Time	*Single* Action Items	Type	Done
1.	_____	_____	_____	☐
2.	_____	_____	_____	☐
3.	_____	_____	_____	☐

90-Day Run

JOURNAL

DAY
31

Strengths: _____

_____

_____

Weaknesses: _____

_____

_____

How I Can Improve: _____

_____

_____

GREAT thoughts for today: _____

_____

_____

Think GREAT Today:

*The more specific you can be about your goals,
the more likely you are to accomplish them.*

90-Day Run

DAILY ACTION PLANNER

DAY
32

	Time	*Multiple* Action Items	Type	Done
1.				☐
2.				☐
3.				☐
4.				☐
5.				☐
6.				☐
7.				☐
8.				☐
9.				☐
10.				☐

	Time	*Single* Action Items	Type	Done
1.				☐
2.				☐
3.				☐

90-Day Run

JOURNAL

DAY
32

Strengths: _____

_____

_____

Weaknesses: _____

_____

_____

How I Can Improve: _____

_____

_____

GREAT thoughts for today: _____

_____

_____

Think GREAT Today:

*Challenging goals cause you to discover
your untapped potential.*

DAILY ACTION PLANNER

DAY
33

	Time	*Multiple* Action Items	Type	Done
1.	_____	_____	_____	☐
2.	_____	_____	_____	☐
3.	_____	_____	_____	☐
4.	_____	_____	_____	☐
5.	_____	_____	_____	☐
6.	_____	_____	_____	☐
7.	_____	_____	_____	☐
8.	_____	_____	_____	☐
9.	_____	_____	_____	☐
10.	_____	_____	_____	☐

	Time	*Single* Action Items	Type	Done
1.	_____	_____	_____	☐
2.	_____	_____	_____	☐
3.	_____	_____	_____	☐

90-Day Run

JOURNAL

DAY
33

Strengths: _____

_____

_____

Weaknesses: _____

_____

_____

How I Can Improve: _____

_____

_____

GREAT thoughts for today: _____

_____

_____

Think GREAT Today:

*Short-term goals give you the immediate motivation
needed to stay on course.*

90-Day Run

DAILY ACTION PLANNER

DAY
34

	Time	*Multiple* Action Items	Type	Done
1.				☐
2.				☐
3.				☐
4.				☐
5.				☐
6.				☐
7.				☐
8.				☐
9.				☐
10.				☐

	Time	*Single* Action Items	Type	Done
1.				☐
2.				☐
3.				☐

90-Day Run

JOURNAL

DAY
34

Strengths: _____

_____

_____

Weaknesses: _____

_____

_____

How I Can Improve: _____

_____

_____

GREAT thoughts for today: _____

_____

_____

Think GREAT Today:

A goal without a reason is like a car without an engine...
it goes nowhere.

DAILY ACTION PLANNER

DAY
35

	Time	*Multiple* Action Items	Type	Done
1.				☐
2.				☐
3.				☐
4.				☐
5.				☐
6.				☐
7.				☐
8.				☐
9.				☐
10.				☐

	Time	*Single* Action Items	Type	Done
1.				☐
2.				☐
3.				☐

90-Day Run

JOURNAL

DAY
35

Strengths: _____

_____

_____

Weaknesses: _____

_____

_____

How I Can Improve: _____

_____

_____

GREAT thoughts for today: _____

_____

_____

Think GREAT Today:

The strength of your reasons determines
your success.

90-Day Run

DAILY ACTION PLANNER

DAY
36

	Time	*Multiple* Action Items	Type	Done
1.				☐
2.				☐
3.				☐
4.				☐
5.				☐
6.				☐
7.				☐
8.				☐
9.				☐
10.				☐

	Time	*Single* Action Items	Type	Done
1.				☐
2.				☐
3.				☐

90-Day Run

JOURNAL

DAY
36

Strengths: _____

_____

_____

Weaknesses: _____

_____

_____

How I Can Improve: _____

_____

_____

GREAT thoughts for today: _____

_____

_____

Think GREAT Today:

Invest your time with people
who will help you to achieve a remarkable life.

90-Day Run

DAILY ACTION PLANNER

DAY
37

	Time	*Multiple* Action Items	Type	Done
1.	_____	_____	_____	☐
2.	_____	_____	_____	☐
3.	_____	_____	_____	☐
4.	_____	_____	_____	☐
5.	_____	_____	_____	☐
6.	_____	_____	_____	☐
7.	_____	_____	_____	☐
8.	_____	_____	_____	☐
9.	_____	_____	_____	☐
10.	_____	_____	_____	☐

	Time	*Single* Action Items	Type	Done
1.	_____	_____	_____	☐
2.	_____	_____	_____	☐
3.	_____	_____	_____	☐

90-Day Run

JOURNAL

DAY
37

Strengths: _____

_____

_____

Weaknesses: _____

_____

_____

How I Can Improve: _____

_____

_____

GREAT thoughts for today: _____

_____

_____

Think GREAT Today:

You cannot recapture yesterday, and tomorrow never comes.
All you have is today.

90-Day Run

DAILY ACTION PLANNER

DAY
38

	Time	*Multiple* Action Items	Type	Done
1.				☐
2.				☐
3.				☐
4.				☐
5.				☐
6.				☐
7.				☐
8.				☐
9.				☐
10.				☐

	Time	*Single* Action Items	Type	Done
1.				☐
2.				☐
3.				☐

90-Day Run

JOURNAL

DAY
38

Strengths: _____
_____
_____

Weaknesses: _____
_____
_____

How I Can Improve: _____
_____
_____

GREAT thoughts for today: _____
_____
_____

Think GREAT Today:

A greater life takes time. Be patiently persistent.

90-Day Run

DAILY ACTION PLANNER

DAY
39

	Time	*Multiple* Action Items	Type	Done
1.				☐
2.				☐
3.				☐
4.				☐
5.				☐
6.				☐
7.				☐
8.				☐
9.				☐
10.				☐

	Time	*Single* Action Items	Type	Done
1.				☐
2.				☐
3.				☐

90-Day Run

JOURNAL

DAY
39

Strengths: _____

_____

_____

Weaknesses: _____

_____

_____

How I Can Improve: _____

_____

_____

GREAT thoughts for today: _____

_____

_____

Think GREAT Today:

Plan out your day, the night before.

DAILY ACTION PLANNER

DAY
40

	Time	*Multiple* Action Items	Type	Done
1.	_____	_____	_____	☐
2.	_____	_____	_____	☐
3.	_____	_____	_____	☐
4.	_____	_____	_____	☐
5.	_____	_____	_____	☐
6.	_____	_____	_____	☐
7.	_____	_____	_____	☐
8.	_____	_____	_____	☐
9.	_____	_____	_____	☐
10.	_____	_____	_____	☐

	Time	*Single* Action Items	Type	Done
1.	_____	_____	_____	☐
2.	_____	_____	_____	☐
3.	_____	_____	_____	☐

90-Day Run

JOURNAL

DAY
40

Strengths: _____

_____

_____

Weaknesses: _____

_____

_____

How I Can Improve: _____

_____

_____

GREAT thoughts for today: _____

_____

_____

Think GREAT Today:

The direction you head in life is
entirely up to you.

DAILY ACTION PLANNER

DAY
41

Time	_Multiple_ Action Items	Type	Done
1.			☐
2.			☐
3.			☐
4.			☐
5.			☐
6.			☐
7.			☐
8.			☐
9.			☐
10.			☐

Time	_Single_ Action Items	Type	Done
1.			☐
2.			☐
3.			☐

90-Day Run

JOURNAL

DAY
41

Strengths: _____

_____

_____

Weaknesses: _____

_____

_____

How I Can Improve: _____

_____

_____

GREAT thoughts for today: _____

_____

_____

Think GREAT Today:

No matter how challenging it gets, never give up.

90-Day Run

DAILY ACTION PLANNER

DAY
42

	Time	*Multiple* Action Items	Type	Done
1.				☐
2.				☐
3.				☐
4.				☐
5.				☐
6.				☐
7.				☐
8.				☐
9.				☐
10.				☐

	Time	*Single* Action Items	Type	Done
1.				☐
2.				☐
3.				☐

90-Day Run

JOURNAL

DAY
42

Strengths: _____

_____

_____

Weaknesses: _____

_____

_____

How I Can Improve: _____

_____

_____

GREAT thoughts for today: _____

_____

_____

Think GREAT Today:

*You need great vision to see what does not
yet exist in your life.*

90-Day Run

DAILY ACTION PLANNER

DAY
43

	Time	*Multiple* Action Items	Type	Done
1.	_____	_____	_____	☐
2.	_____	_____	_____	☐
3.	_____	_____	_____	☐
4.	_____	_____	_____	☐
5.	_____	_____	_____	☐
6.	_____	_____	_____	☐
7.	_____	_____	_____	☐
8.	_____	_____	_____	☐
9.	_____	_____	_____	☐
10.	_____	_____	_____	☐

	Time	*Single* Action Items	Type	Done
1.	_____	_____	_____	☐
2.	_____	_____	_____	☐
3.	_____	_____	_____	☐

90-Day Run

JOURNAL

DAY
43

Strengths: _____

_____

_____

Weaknesses: _____

_____

_____

How I Can Improve: _____

_____

_____

GREAT thoughts for today: _____

_____

_____

Think GREAT Today:

Focus on the things you are most grateful for.

90-Day Run

DAILY ACTION PLANNER

DAY
44

	Time	*Multiple* Action Items	Type	Done
1.				☐
2.				☐
3.				☐
4.				☐
5.				☐
6.				☐
7.				☐
8.				☐
9.				☐
10.				☐

	Time	*Single* Action Items	Type	Done
1.				☐
2.				☐
3.				☐

90-Day Run

JOURNAL

DAY
44

Strengths: _____

_____

_____

Weaknesses: _____

_____

_____

How I Can Improve: _____

_____

_____

GREAT thoughts for today: _____

_____

_____

Think GREAT Today:

*When you focus on a GREAT future,
it positively impacts each day.*

DAILY ACTION PLANNER

DAY
45

	Time	*Multiple* Action Items	Type	Done
1.	_____	_____	_____	☐
2.	_____	_____	_____	☐
3.	_____	_____	_____	☐
4.	_____	_____	_____	☐
5.	_____	_____	_____	☐
6.	_____	_____	_____	☐
7.	_____	_____	_____	☐
8.	_____	_____	_____	☐
9.	_____	_____	_____	☐
10.	_____	_____	_____	☐

	Time	*Single* Action Items	Type	Done
1.	_____	_____	_____	☐
2.	_____	_____	_____	☐
3.	_____	_____	_____	☐

90-Day Run

JOURNAL

DAY
45

Strengths: _____

_____

_____

Weaknesses: _____

_____

_____

How I Can Improve: _____

_____

_____

GREAT thoughts for today: _____

_____

_____

Think GREAT Today:

*Greatness happens when you do what the average person
never gets around to.*

90-Day Run

DAILY ACTION PLANNER

DAY
46

	Time	*Multiple* Action Items	Type	Done
1.				☐
2.				☐
3.				☐
4.				☐
5.				☐
6.				☐
7.				☐
8.				☐
9.				☐
10.				☐

	Time	*Single* Action Items	Type	Done
1.				☐
2.				☐
3.				☐

90-Day Run

JOURNAL

DAY
46

Strengths: _____

_____

_____

Weaknesses: _____

_____

_____

How I Can Improve: _____

_____

_____

GREAT thoughts for today: _____

_____

_____

Think GREAT Today:

Never stop dreaming.

90-Day Run

DAILY ACTION PLANNER

DAY
47

	Time	*Multiple* Action Items	Type	Done
1.				☐
2.				☐
3.				☐
4.				☐
5.				☐
6.				☐
7.				☐
8.				☐
9.				☐
10.				☐

	Time	*Single* Action Items	Type	Done
1.				☐
2.				☐
3.				☐

90-Day Run

JOURNAL

DAY
47

Strengths: _____

_____

_____

Weaknesses: _____

_____

_____

How I Can Improve: _____

_____

_____

GREAT thoughts for today: _____

_____

_____

Think GREAT Today:

*Think of all the people who will benefit
from your accomplished goals.*

90-Day Run

DAILY ACTION PLANNER

DAY
48

	Time	*Multiple* Action Items	Type	Done
1.	_____	_____	_____	☐
2.	_____	_____	_____	☐
3.	_____	_____	_____	☐
4.	_____	_____	_____	☐
5.	_____	_____	_____	☐
6.	_____	_____	_____	☐
7.	_____	_____	_____	☐
8.	_____	_____	_____	☐
9.	_____	_____	_____	☐
10.	_____	_____	_____	☐

	Time	*Single* Action Items	Type	Done
1.	_____	_____	_____	☐
2.	_____	_____	_____	☐
3.	_____	_____	_____	☐

90-Day Run

JOURNAL

DAY
48

Strengths: _____

_____

_____

Weaknesses: _____

_____

_____

How I Can Improve: _____

_____

_____

GREAT thoughts for today: _____

_____

_____

Think GREAT Today:

Today, focus on the greater purpose of your life.

90-Day Run

DAILY ACTION PLANNER

DAY
49

	Time	*Multiple* Action Items	Type	Done
1.				☐
2.				☐
3.				☐
4.				☐
5.				☐
6.				☐
7.				☐
8.				☐
9.				☐
10.				☐

	Time	*Single* Action Items	Type	Done
1.				☐
2.				☐
3.				☐

90-Day Run

JOURNAL

DAY
49

Strengths: _____

_____

_____

Weaknesses: _____

_____

_____

How I Can Improve: _____

_____

_____

GREAT thoughts for today: _____

_____

_____

Think GREAT Today:

You are creating your own destiny.

90-Day Run

DAILY ACTION PLANNER

DAY
50

	Time	*Multiple* Action Items	Type	Done
1.	_____	_____	_____	☐
2.	_____	_____	_____	☐
3.	_____	_____	_____	☐
4.	_____	_____	_____	☐
5.	_____	_____	_____	☐
6.	_____	_____	_____	☐
7.	_____	_____	_____	☐
8.	_____	_____	_____	☐
9.	_____	_____	_____	☐
10.	_____	_____	_____	☐

	Time	*Single* Action Items	Type	Done
1.	_____	_____	_____	☐
2.	_____	_____	_____	☐
3.	_____	_____	_____	☐

90-Day Run

JOURNAL

DAY
50

Strengths: _____
_____
_____

Weaknesses: _____
_____
_____

How I Can Improve: _____
_____
_____

GREAT thoughts for today: _____
_____
_____

Think GREAT Today:

*What impact do you want to have on the
people who matter the most to you?*

90-Day Run

DAILY ACTION PLANNER

DAY
51

	Time	*Multiple* Action Items	Type	Done
1.				☐
2.				☐
3.				☐
4.				☐
5.				☐
6.				☐
7.				☐
8.				☐
9.				☐
10.				☐

	Time	*Single* Action Items	Type	Done
1.				☐
2.				☐
3.				☐

90-Day Run

JOURNAL

DAY
51

Strengths: _____

_____

_____

Weaknesses: _____

_____

_____

How I Can Improve: _____

_____

_____

GREAT thoughts for today: _____

_____

_____

Think GREAT Today:

When you extend greatness beyond yourself,
there is no limit to what you can accomplish.

90-Day Run

DAILY ACTION PLANNER

DAY
52

	Time	*Multiple* Action Items	Type	Done
1.				☐
2.				☐
3.				☐
4.				☐
5.				☐
6.				☐
7.				☐
8.				☐
9.				☐
10.				☐

	Time	*Single* Action Items	Type	Done
1.				☐
2.				☐
3.				☐

90-Day Run

JOURNAL

DAY
52

Strengths: _____

_____

_____

Weaknesses: _____

_____

_____

How I Can Improve: _____

_____

_____

GREAT thoughts for today: _____

_____

_____

Think GREAT Today:

*It is healthy to stop focusing on yourself
and start helping others to succeed.*

90-Day Run

DAILY ACTION PLANNER

DAY
53

	Time	*Multiple* Action Items	Type	Done
1.				☐
2.				☐
3.				☐
4.				☐
5.				☐
6.				☐
7.				☐
8.				☐
9.				☐
10.				☐

	Time	*Single* Action Items	Type	Done
1.				☐
2.				☐
3.				☐

90-Day Run

JOURNAL

DAY
53

Strengths: _____

_____

_____

Weaknesses: _____

_____

_____

How I Can Improve: _____

_____

_____

GREAT thoughts for today: _____

_____

_____

Think GREAT Today:

If someone else can do it, so can you.

DAILY ACTION PLANNER

DAY
54

	Time	*Multiple* Action Items	Type	Done
1.				☐
2.				☐
3.				☐
4.				☐
5.				☐
6.				☐
7.				☐
8.				☐
9.				☐
10.				☐

	Time	*Single* Action Items	Type	Done
1.				☐
2.				☐
3.				☐

90-Day Run

JOURNAL

DAY
54

Strengths: _____

_____

_____

Weaknesses: _____

_____

_____

How I Can Improve: _____

_____

_____

GREAT thoughts for today: _____

_____

_____

Think GREAT Today:

To keep your belief level strong,
repeat powerful affirmations to yourself.

DAILY ACTION PLANNER

DAY
55

	Time	*Multiple* Action Items	Type	Done
1.	_____	_____	____	☐
2.	_____	_____	____	☐
3.	_____	_____	____	☐
4.	_____	_____	____	☐
5.	_____	_____	____	☐
6.	_____	_____	____	☐
7.	_____	_____	____	☐
8.	_____	_____	____	☐
9.	_____	_____	____	☐
10.	_____	_____	____	☐

	Time	*Single* Action Items	Type	Done
1.	_____	_____	____	☐
2.	_____	_____	____	☐
3.	_____	_____	____	☐

90-Day Run

JOURNAL

DAY
55

Strengths: _____

_____

_____

Weaknesses: _____

_____

_____

How I Can Improve: _____

_____

_____

GREAT thoughts for today: _____

_____

_____

Think GREAT Today:

Take 100% responsibility for your life.

90-Day Run

DAILY ACTION PLANNER

DAY
56

	Time	*Multiple* Action Items	Type	Done
1.				☐
2.				☐
3.				☐
4.				☐
5.				☐
6.				☐
7.				☐
8.				☐
9.				☐
10.				☐

	Time	*Single* Action Items	Type	Done
1.				☐
2.				☐
3.				☐

90-Day Run

JOURNAL

DAY
56

Strengths: _____

_____

_____

Weaknesses: _____

_____

_____

How I Can Improve: _____

_____

_____

GREAT thoughts for today: _____

_____

_____

Think GREAT Today:

*Announcing your goals to more people will
increase your desire to accomplish them.*

90-Day Run

DAILY ACTION PLANNER

DAY
57

	Time	*Multiple* Action Items	Type	Done
1.	_____	_____	_____	☐
2.	_____	_____	_____	☐
3.	_____	_____	_____	☐
4.	_____	_____	_____	☐
5.	_____	_____	_____	☐
6.	_____	_____	_____	☐
7.	_____	_____	_____	☐
8.	_____	_____	_____	☐
9.	_____	_____	_____	☐
10.	_____	_____	_____	☐

	Time	*Single* Action Items	Type	Done
1.	_____	_____	_____	☐
2.	_____	_____	_____	☐
3.	_____	_____	_____	☐

90-Day Run

JOURNAL

DAY
57

Strengths: _____

_____

_____

Weaknesses: _____

_____

_____

How I Can Improve: _____

_____

_____

GREAT thoughts for today: _____

_____

_____

Think GREAT Today:

Greatness is absolutely attainable,
no matter what circumstances you face.

90-Day Run

DAILY ACTION PLANNER

DAY
58

	Time	*Multiple* Action Items	Type	Done
1.				☐
2.				☐
3.				☐
4.				☐
5.				☐
6.				☐
7.				☐
8.				☐
9.				☐
10.				☐

	Time	*Single* Action Items	Type	Done
1.				☐
2.				☐
3.				☐

90-Day Run

JOURNAL

DAY
58

Strengths: _____

_____

_____

Weaknesses: _____

_____

_____

How I Can Improve: _____

_____

_____

GREAT thoughts for today: _____

_____

_____

Think GREAT Today:

*Strong reasons allow you to turn your personal energy
into personal action.*

90-Day Run

DAILY ACTION PLANNER

DAY
59

	Time	*Multiple* Action Items	Type	Done
1.				☐
2.				☐
3.				☐
4.				☐
5.				☐
6.				☐
7.				☐
8.				☐
9.				☐
10.				☐

	Time	*Single* Action Items	Type	Done
1.				☐
2.				☐
3.				☐

90-Day Run

JOURNAL

DAY
59

Strengths: _____

_____

_____

Weaknesses: _____

_____

_____

How I Can Improve: _____

_____

_____

GREAT thoughts for today: _____

_____

_____

Think GREAT Today:

Having high expectations on yourself will
move you from status quo to status grow.

90-Day Run

DAILY ACTION PLANNER

DAY
60

	Time	*Multiple* Action Items	Type	Done
1.				☐
2.				☐
3.				☐
4.				☐
5.				☐
6.				☐
7.				☐
8.				☐
9.				☐
10.				☐

	Time	*Single* Action Items	Type	Done
1.				☐
2.				☐
3.				☐

90-Day Run

JOURNAL

DAY
60

Strengths: _____

_____

_____

Weaknesses: _____

_____

_____

How I Can Improve: _____

_____

_____

GREAT thoughts for today: _____

_____

_____

Think GREAT Today:

You can always control your thoughts and your actions.

90-Day Run

DAILY ACTION PLANNER

DAY
61

	Time	*Multiple* Action Items	Type	Done
1.				☐
2.				☐
3.				☐
4.				☐
5.				☐
6.				☐
7.				☐
8.				☐
9.				☐
10.				☐

	Time	*Single* Action Items	Type	Done
1.				☐
2.				☐
3.				☐

90-Day Run

JOURNAL

DAY
61

Strengths: _____

_____

_____

Weaknesses: _____

_____

_____

How I Can Improve: _____

_____

_____

GREAT thoughts for today: _____

_____

_____

Think GREAT Today:

You only fail if you quit.

DAILY ACTION PLANNER

DAY
62

	Time	*Multiple* Action Items	Type	Done
1.				☐
2.				☐
3.				☐
4.				☐
5.				☐
6.				☐
7.				☐
8.				☐
9.				☐
10.				☐

	Time	*Single* Action Items	Type	Done
1.				☐
2.				☐
3.				☐

90-Day Run

JOURNAL

DAY
62

Strengths: _____

_____

_____

Weaknesses: _____

_____

_____

How I Can Improve: _____

_____

_____

GREAT thoughts for today: _____

_____

_____

Think GREAT Today:

Now is the best time to take action.

90-Day Run

DAILY ACTION PLANNER

DAY
63

	Time	*Multiple* Action Items	Type	Done
1.				☐
2.				☐
3.				☐
4.				☐
5.				☐
6.				☐
7.				☐
8.				☐
9.				☐
10.				☐

	Time	*Single* Action Items	Type	Done
1.				☐
2.				☐
3.				☐

90-Day Run

JOURNAL

DAY
63

Strengths: _____

_____

_____

Weaknesses: _____

_____

_____

How I Can Improve: _____

_____

_____

GREAT thoughts for today: _____

_____

_____

Think GREAT Today:

*There is a big difference between knowing
what to do and actually doing it.*

90-Day Run

DAILY ACTION PLANNER

DAY
64

	Time	*Multiple* Action Items	Type	Done
1.				☐
2.				☐
3.				☐
4.				☐
5.				☐
6.				☐
7.				☐
8.				☐
9.				☐
10.				☐

	Time	*Single* Action Items	Type	Done
1.				☐
2.				☐
3.				☐

90-Day Run

JOURNAL

DAY
64

Strengths: _____

_____

_____

Weaknesses: _____

_____

_____

How I Can Improve: _____

_____

_____

GREAT thoughts for today: _____

_____

_____

Think GREAT Today:

Taking small steps is better than taking no steps at all.

90-Day Run

DAILY ACTION PLANNER

DAY
65

	Time	*Multiple* Action Items	Type	Done
1.				☐
2.				☐
3.				☐
4.				☐
5.				☐
6.				☐
7.				☐
8.				☐
9.				☐
10.				☐

	Time	*Single* Action Items	Type	Done
1.				☐
2.				☐
3.				☐

90-Day Run

JOURNAL

DAY
65

Strengths: _____

_____

_____

Weaknesses: _____

_____

_____

How I Can Improve: _____

_____

_____

GREAT thoughts for today: _____

_____

_____

Think GREAT Today:

Your mind has already created your goals,
all you need to do is to take the right actions.

90-Day Run

DAILY ACTION PLANNER

DAY
66

	Time	*Multiple* Action Items	Type	Done
1.				☐
2.				☐
3.				☐
4.				☐
5.				☐
6.				☐
7.				☐
8.				☐
9.				☐
10.				☐

	Time	*Single* Action Items	Type	Done
1.				☐
2.				☐
3.				☐

90-Day Run

JOURNAL

DAY
66

Strengths: _____

_____

_____

Weaknesses: _____

_____

_____

How I Can Improve: _____

_____

_____

GREAT thoughts for today: _____

_____

_____

Think GREAT Today:

*Track your progress and make the necessary
course corrections.*

DAILY ACTION PLANNER

DAY
67

	Time	*Multiple* Action Items	Type	Done
1.				☐
2.				☐
3.				☐
4.				☐
5.				☐
6.				☐
7.				☐
8.				☐
9.				☐
10.				☐

	Time	*Single* Action Items	Type	Done
1.				☐
2.				☐
3.				☐

90-Day Run

JOURNAL

DAY
67

Strengths: _____

_____

_____

Weaknesses: _____

_____

_____

How I Can Improve: _____

_____

_____

GREAT thoughts for today: _____

_____

_____

Think GREAT Today:

Personal accountability changes your perceptions
about what you can accomplish.

DAILY ACTION PLANNER

DAY
68

	Time	*Multiple* Action Items	Type	Done
1.	_____	_____	_____	☐
2.	_____	_____	_____	☐
3.	_____	_____	_____	☐
4.	_____	_____	_____	☐
5.	_____	_____	_____	☐
6.	_____	_____	_____	☐
7.	_____	_____	_____	☐
8.	_____	_____	_____	☐
9.	_____	_____	_____	☐
10.	_____	_____	_____	☐

	Time	*Single* Action Items	Type	Done
1.	_____	_____	_____	☐
2.	_____	_____	_____	☐
3.	_____	_____	_____	☐

90-Day Run

JOURNAL

DAY
68

Strengths: _____

_____

_____

Weaknesses: _____

_____

_____

How I Can Improve: _____

_____

_____

GREAT thoughts for today: _____

_____

_____

Think GREAT Today:

People who track their results, discuss their progress.
People who fail to track their results, discuss their problems.

90-Day Run

DAILY ACTION PLANNER

DAY
69

	Time	*Multiple* Action Items	Type	Done
1.				☐
2.				☐
3.				☐
4.				☐
5.				☐
6.				☐
7.				☐
8.				☐
9.				☐
10.				☐

	Time	*Single* Action Items	Type	Done
1.				☐
2.				☐
3.				☐

90-Day Run

JOURNAL

DAY
69

Strengths: _____

_____

_____

Weaknesses: _____

_____

_____

How I Can Improve: _____

_____

_____

GREAT thoughts for today: _____

_____

_____

Think GREAT Today:

Time is a commodity that you cannot get back.
Do not waste time today.

90-Day Run

DAILY ACTION PLANNER

DAY
70

	Time	*Multiple* Action Items	Type	Done
1.				☐
2.				☐
3.				☐
4.				☐
5.				☐
6.				☐
7.				☐
8.				☐
9.				☐
10.				☐

	Time	*Single* Action Items	Type	Done
1.				☐
2.				☐
3.				☐

90-Day Run

JOURNAL

DAY
70

Strengths: _____

_____

_____

Weaknesses: _____

_____

_____

How I Can Improve: _____

_____

_____

GREAT thoughts for today: _____

_____

_____

Think GREAT Today:

Tracking your results will improve your performance.

90-Day Run

DAILY ACTION PLANNER

DAY
71

	Time	*Multiple* Action Items	Type	Done
1.				☐
2.				☐
3.				☐
4.				☐
5.				☐
6.				☐
7.				☐
8.				☐
9.				☐
10.				☐

	Time	*Single* Action Items	Type	Done
1.				☐
2.				☐
3.				☐

90-Day Run

JOURNAL

DAY
71

Strengths: _____

_____

_____

Weaknesses: _____

_____

_____

How I Can Improve: _____

_____

_____

GREAT thoughts for today: _____

_____

_____

Think GREAT Today:

Having the right mindset moves you forward.

90-Day Run

DAILY ACTION PLANNER

DAY
72

Time	*Multiple* Action Items	Type	Done
1.			☐
2.			☐
3.			☐
4.			☐
5.			☐
6.			☐
7.			☐
8.			☐
9.			☐
10.			☐

Time	*Single* Action Items	Type	Done
1.			☐
2.			☐
3.			☐

90-Day Run

JOURNAL

DAY
72

Strengths: _____

_____

_____

Weaknesses: _____

_____

_____

How I Can Improve: _____

_____

_____

GREAT thoughts for today: _____

_____

_____

Think GREAT Today:

*Having a deep passion will move you
beyond your obstacles.*

90-Day Run

DAILY ACTION PLANNER

DAY
73

	Time	*Multiple* Action Items	Type	Done
1.	_____	_____	_____	☐
2.	_____	_____	_____	☐
3.	_____	_____	_____	☐
4.	_____	_____	_____	☐
5.	_____	_____	_____	☐
6.	_____	_____	_____	☐
7.	_____	_____	_____	☐
8.	_____	_____	_____	☐
9.	_____	_____	_____	☐
10.	_____	_____	_____	☐

	Time	*Single* Action Items	Type	Done
1.	_____	_____	_____	☐
2.	_____	_____	_____	☐
3.	_____	_____	_____	☐

90-Day Run

JOURNAL

DAY
73

Strengths: _____

_____

_____

Weaknesses: _____

_____

_____

How I Can Improve: _____

_____

_____

GREAT thoughts for today: _____

_____

_____

Think GREAT Today:

Greatness requires dedication, effort, time, and sacrifices.

DAILY ACTION PLANNER

DAY
74

	Time	*Multiple* Action Items	Type	Done
1.	_____	_____	_____	☐
2.	_____	_____	_____	☐
3.	_____	_____	_____	☐
4.	_____	_____	_____	☐
5.	_____	_____	_____	☐
6.	_____	_____	_____	☐
7.	_____	_____	_____	☐
8.	_____	_____	_____	☐
9.	_____	_____	_____	☐
10.	_____	_____	_____	☐

	Time	*Single* Action Items	Type	Done
1.	_____	_____	_____	☐
2.	_____	_____	_____	☐
3.	_____	_____	_____	☐

90-Day Run

JOURNAL

DAY
74

Strengths: _____

_____

_____

Weaknesses: _____

_____

_____

How I Can Improve: _____

_____

_____

GREAT thoughts for today: _____

_____

_____

Think GREAT Today:

Accomplishing great goals is not always easy,
but nothing of significance ever is.

90-Day Run

DAILY ACTION PLANNER

DAY
75

	Time	*Multiple* Action Items	Type	Done
1.				☐
2.				☐
3.				☐
4.				☐
5.				☐
6.				☐
7.				☐
8.				☐
9.				☐
10.				☐

	Time	*Single* Action Items	Type	Done
1.				☐
2.				☐
3.				☐

90-Day Run

JOURNAL

DAY
75

Strengths: _____

_____

_____

Weaknesses: _____

_____

_____

How I Can Improve: _____

_____

_____

GREAT thoughts for today: _____

_____

_____

Think GREAT Today:

*What is your definition of a
greater life?*

90-Day Run

DAILY ACTION PLANNER

DAY
76

	Time	*Multiple* Action Items	Type	Done
1.				☐
2.				☐
3.				☐
4.				☐
5.				☐
6.				☐
7.				☐
8.				☐
9.				☐
10.				☐

	Time	*Single* Action Items	Type	Done
1.				☐
2.				☐
3.				☐

90-Day Run

JOURNAL

DAY
76

Strengths: _____

_____

_____

Weaknesses: _____

_____

_____

How I Can Improve: _____

_____

_____

GREAT thoughts for today: _____

_____

_____

Think GREAT Today:

Can you empower someone else today?

90-Day Run

DAILY ACTION PLANNER

DAY
77

	Time	*Multiple* Action Items	Type	Done
1.	_____	_____	_____	☐
2.	_____	_____	_____	☐
3.	_____	_____	_____	☐
4.	_____	_____	_____	☐
5.	_____	_____	_____	☐
6.	_____	_____	_____	☐
7.	_____	_____	_____	☐
8.	_____	_____	_____	☐
9.	_____	_____	_____	☐
10.	_____	_____	_____	☐

	Time	*Single* Action Items	Type	Done
1.	_____	_____	_____	☐
2.	_____	_____	_____	☐
3.	_____	_____	_____	☐

90-Day Run

JOURNAL

DAY
77

Strengths: _____

_____

_____

Weaknesses: _____

_____

_____

How I Can Improve: _____

_____

_____

GREAT thoughts for today: _____

_____

_____

Think GREAT Today:

Your life deserves greatness, doesn't it?

90-Day Run

DAILY ACTION PLANNER

DAY
78

	Time	*Multiple* Action Items	Type	Done
1.	_____	_____	_____	☐
2.	_____	_____	_____	☐
3.	_____	_____	_____	☐
4.	_____	_____	_____	☐
5.	_____	_____	_____	☐
6.	_____	_____	_____	☐
7.	_____	_____	_____	☐
8.	_____	_____	_____	☐
9.	_____	_____	_____	☐
10.	_____	_____	_____	☐

	Time	*Single* Action Items	Type	Done
1.	_____	_____	_____	☐
2.	_____	_____	_____	☐
3.	_____	_____	_____	☐

90-Day Run

JOURNAL

DAY
78

Strengths: _____

_____

_____

Weaknesses: _____

_____

_____

How I Can Improve: _____

_____

_____

GREAT thoughts for today: _____

_____

_____

Think GREAT Today:

Your patterns and habits got you to where you are today.
Your new patterns and habits will get you to where you need to be.

90-Day Run

DAILY ACTION PLANNER

DAY
79

	Time	*Multiple* Action Items	Type	Done
1.	_____	_____	_____	☐
2.	_____	_____	_____	☐
3.	_____	_____	_____	☐
4.	_____	_____	_____	☐
5.	_____	_____	_____	☐
6.	_____	_____	_____	☐
7.	_____	_____	_____	☐
8.	_____	_____	_____	☐
9.	_____	_____	_____	☐
10.	_____	_____	_____	☐

	Time	*Single* Action Items	Type	Done
1.	_____	_____	_____	☐
2.	_____	_____	_____	☐
3.	_____	_____	_____	☐

JOURNAL

DAY
79

Strengths: _____

_____

_____

Weaknesses: _____

_____

_____

How I Can Improve: _____

_____

_____

GREAT thoughts for today: _____

_____

_____

Think GREAT Today:

If you continue to step forward,
your goals become easier to accomplish.

90-Day Run

DAILY ACTION PLANNER

DAY
80

	Time	*Multiple* Action Items	Type	Done
1.	_____	_____	_____	☐
2.	_____	_____	_____	☐
3.	_____	_____	_____	☐
4.	_____	_____	_____	☐
5.	_____	_____	_____	☐
6.	_____	_____	_____	☐
7.	_____	_____	_____	☐
8.	_____	_____	_____	☐
9.	_____	_____	_____	☐
10.	_____	_____	_____	☐

	Time	*Single* Action Items	Type	Done
1.	_____	_____	_____	☐
2.	_____	_____	_____	☐
3.	_____	_____	_____	☐

90-Day Run

JOURNAL

DAY
80

Strengths: _____

_____

_____

Weaknesses: _____

_____

_____

How I Can Improve: _____

_____

_____

GREAT thoughts for today: _____

_____

_____

Think GREAT Today:

Most people are ready for a greater life,
but few are prepared.

90-Day Run

DAILY ACTION PLANNER

DAY
81

	Time	*Multiple* Action Items	Type	Done
1.				☐
2.				☐
3.				☐
4.				☐
5.				☐
6.				☐
7.				☐
8.				☐
9.				☐
10.				☐

	Time	*Single* Action Items	Type	Done
1.				☐
2.				☐
3.				☐

90-Day Run

JOURNAL

DAY
81

Strengths: _____

_____

_____

Weaknesses: _____

_____

_____

How I Can Improve: _____

_____

_____

GREAT thoughts for today: _____

_____

_____

Think GREAT Today:

There is no limit to what you can accomplish in your life.

90-Day Run

DAILY ACTION PLANNER

DAY
82

	Time	*Multiple* Action Items	Type	Done
1.				☐
2.				☐
3.				☐
4.				☐
5.				☐
6.				☐
7.				☐
8.				☐
9.				☐
10.				☐

	Time	*Single* Action Items	Type	Done
1.				☐
2.				☐
3.				☐

90-Day Run

JOURNAL

DAY
82

Strengths: _____

_____

_____

Weaknesses: _____

_____

_____

How I Can Improve: _____

_____

_____

GREAT thoughts for today: _____

_____

_____

Think GREAT Today:

Even a great wind cannot move a boat which is tied to the dock.
Untie yourself and raise your sails.

90-Day Run

DAILY ACTION PLANNER

DAY
83

	Time	*Multiple* Action Items	Type	Done
1.				☐
2.				☐
3.				☐
4.				☐
5.				☐
6.				☐
7.				☐
8.				☐
9.				☐
10.				☐

	Time	*Single* Action Items	Type	Done
1.				☐
2.				☐
3.				☐

90-Day Run

JOURNAL

DAY
83

Strengths: _____

_____

_____

Weaknesses: _____

_____

_____

How I Can Improve: _____

_____

_____

GREAT thoughts for today: _____

_____

_____

Think GREAT Today:

*As you pursue a greater life, strive to
find balance.*

90-Day Run

DAILY ACTION PLANNER

DAY
84

	Time	*Multiple* Action Items	Type	Done
1.				☐
2.				☐
3.				☐
4.				☐
5.				☐
6.				☐
7.				☐
8.				☐
9.				☐
10.				☐

	Time	*Single* Action Items	Type	Done
1.				☐
2.				☐
3.				☐

90-Day Run

JOURNAL

DAY
84

Strengths: _____

_____

_____

Weaknesses: _____

_____

_____

How I Can Improve: _____

_____

_____

GREAT thoughts for today: _____

_____

_____

Think GREAT Today:

Do not chase perfection; pursue progress.

90-Day Run

DAILY ACTION PLANNER

DAY
85

	Time	_Multiple_ Action Items	Type	Done
1.				☐
2.				☐
3.				☐
4.				☐
5.				☐
6.				☐
7.				☐
8.				☐
9.				☐
10.				☐

	Time	_Single_ Action Items	Type	Done
1.				☐
2.				☐
3.				☐

90-Day Run

JOURNAL

DAY
85

Strengths: _____

_____

_____

Weaknesses: _____

_____

_____

How I Can Improve: _____

_____

_____

GREAT thoughts for today: _____

_____

_____

Think GREAT Today:

Everyone has 24 hours in their day.
What will you do with your time today?

90-Day Run

DAILY ACTION PLANNER

DAY
86

	Time	*Multiple* Action Items	Type	Done
1.				☐
2.				☐
3.				☐
4.				☐
5.				☐
6.				☐
7.				☐
8.				☐
9.				☐
10.				☐

	Time	*Single* Action Items	Type	Done
1.				☐
2.				☐
3.				☐

90-Day Run

JOURNAL

DAY
86

Strengths: _____

_____

_____

Weaknesses: _____

_____

_____

How I Can Improve: _____

_____

_____

GREAT thoughts for today: _____

_____

_____

Think GREAT Today:

Only one person can stop you from accomplishing your goals - you!

90-Day Run

DAILY ACTION PLANNER

DAY
87

	Time	*Multiple* Action Items	Type	Done
1.				☐
2.				☐
3.				☐
4.				☐
5.				☐
6.				☐
7.				☐
8.				☐
9.				☐
10.				☐

	Time	*Single* Action Items	Type	Done
1.				☐
2.				☐
3.				☐

90-Day Run

JOURNAL

DAY
87

Strengths: _____

_____

_____

Weaknesses: _____

_____

_____

How I Can Improve: _____

_____

_____

GREAT thoughts for today: _____

_____

_____

Think GREAT Today:

GREAT things are in store for you.

DAILY ACTION PLANNER

DAY
88

	Time	*Multiple* Action Items	Type	Done
1.				☐
2.				☐
3.				☐
4.				☐
5.				☐
6.				☐
7.				☐
8.				☐
9.				☐
10.				☐

	Time	*Single* Action Items	Type	Done
1.				☐
2.				☐
3.				☐

90-Day Run

DAY
88

Strengths: _____

_____

_____

Weaknesses: _____

_____

_____

How I Can Improve: _____

_____

_____

GREAT thoughts for today: _____

_____

_____

Think GREAT Today:

Choose to see your life as a gift.

90-Day Run

DAILY ACTION PLANNER

DAY
89

	Time	*Multiple* Action Items	Type	Done
1.				☐
2.				☐
3.				☐
4.				☐
5.				☐
6.				☐
7.				☐
8.				☐
9.				☐
10.				☐

	Time	*Single* Action Items	Type	Done
1.				☐
2.				☐
3.				☐

90-Day Run

JOURNAL

DAY
89

Strengths: _____

_____

_____

Weaknesses: _____

_____

_____

How I Can Improve: _____

_____

_____

GREAT thoughts for today: _____

_____

_____

Think GREAT Today:

You may not be able to change your circumstances,
but you can change how you handle them.

90-Day Run

DAILY ACTION PLANNER

DAY
90

	Time	*Multiple* Action Items	Type	Done
1.				☐
2.				☐
3.				☐
4.				☐
5.				☐
6.				☐
7.				☐
8.				☐
9.				☐
10.				☐

	Time	*Single* Action Items	Type	Done
1.				☐
2.				☐
3.				☐

90-Day Run

JOURNAL

DAY
90

Strengths: _____

_____

_____

Weaknesses: _____

_____

_____

How I Can Improve: _____

_____

_____

GREAT thoughts for today: _____

_____

_____

Think GREAT Today:

You have done an amazing job of staying focused.

90-Day Run

SHORT-TERM GOALS

Congratulations!

GOAL   DATE COMPLETED

1. _____   _____

2. _____   _____

3. _____   _____

4. _____   _____

5. _____   _____

6. _____   _____

7. _____   _____

8. _____   _____

9. _____   _____

10. _____   _____

GREAT Job!

By completing your **90 Day Run**, you have done so much to enhance your life. You have accomplished short-term goals and put yourself on track to accomplishing your long-term goals which will help you to achieve further levels of greatness.

By staying on track for 90 days you have not only made a major impact in your life, but I am confident that you have made an impact in the lives of many others. Use your time in between your **90 Day Runs** to reflect on your accomplishments and focus on other areas of your life you would like to improve.

As you accomplished your goals, you undoubtedly started to think about your new goals which would be life-changing and remarkable in magnitude. Start the habit of linking together your **90 Day Runs** to achieve your long-term goals.

Below, write down five new important goals you need to accomplish on your next **90 Day Run**.

YOUR NEXT 5 IMPORTANT GOALS

1. _____

2. _____

3. _____

4. _____

5. _____

WWW.THINKGREAT90.COM

Please visit our website for additional information to help you and your organization achieve greater results:

- Powerful Products
- Inspirational Seminars
- Interactive Tools
- Events and Appearances with Erik Therwanger
- Register for the free GREAT Thought of the Week

For additional information, please visit
http://www.thinkgreat90.com

Additional books in the Think GREAT® Collection:

- **The GOAL Formula**

- **3–D Sales**

- **The LEADERSHIP Connection**

- **The SCALE Factor**